Individual Sports at the Paralympics

BY MATT BOWERS

Amicus High Interest is published by Amicus and Amicus Ink
P.O. Box 1329, Mankato, MN 56002
www.amicuspublishing.us

Library of Congress Cataloging-in-Publication Data
Names: Bowers, Matt (Matthew David), 1976- author.
Title: Individual sports at the Paralympics / by Matt Bowers.
Other titles: Paralympic sports
Description: Mankato, Minnesota : Amicus/Amicus Ink, [2020] | Series:
  Paralympic sports | Includes bibliographic references
  and index. | Audience: Grades: K-3.
Identifiers: LCCN 2018054511 (print) | LCCN 2019004090
  (ebook) | ISBN 9781681518695 (pdf) | ISBN 9781681518299
  (library binding) | ISBN 9781681525570 (pbk.)
Subjects: LCSH: Paralympic Games—Juvenile literature. | Sports for
  people with disabilities—Juvenile literature. | Athletes with
  disabilities—Juvenile literature.
Classification: LCC GV722.5.P37 (ebook) | LCC GV722.5.P37 B65
  2020 (print) | DDC 796.04/56—dc23
LC record available at https://lccn.loc.gov/2018054511

Editor: Alissa Thielges
Series Designer: Kathleen Petelinsek
Book Designer: Ciara Beitlich
Photo Researchers: Holly Young and Shane Freed

Photo Credits: AP/Jens B'ttner/picture-alliance/dpa cover; AP/Mauro
Pimentel 4; Alamy/dpa picture alliance 7; Alamy/Mark Davidson 8;
Alamy/Michael Preston 10-11; AP/Matt Dunham 12; Alamy/Actionplus
15; Alamy/Marco Ciccolella 16, 29; Newscom/NurPhoto 18-19;
Alamy/Chris Radburn 20; AP/Silvia Izquierdo 23; Alamy/Andrew
Matthews 24; Newscom/Kenjiro Matsuo 26-27

Printed in the United States of America

HC 10 9 8 7 6 5 4 3 2 1
PB 10 9 8 7 6 5 4 3 2 1

Table of Contents

Gyu Dea Kim from South Korea wins the bronze medal in the men's marathon.

The Best of the Best

Are you ready for the Summer Paralympic Games? This is where athletes with a **disability** come from around the world to compete. They are the world's best. With strength and skill, they go for a gold medal. There are many **individual** sports. In these sports, one person tries to be the fastest, strongest, or most precise.

Para Athletics

Ready! Set! Go! Racers dash around a track. On the field, athletes show their strength. Some hurl javelins. These long spears fly far! Other athletes jump as far as they can. This is Para athletics. These track-and-field events have been a part of the Paralympics since 1960. They are some of the most popular sports to watch.

German runner Vanessa Low sprints in a 100-meter event.

Para athletes speed down the track in racing wheelchairs.

 How many Para athletic events are there?

Para athletics has many different **sport classes**. A sport class is a group of athletes. It's based on an athlete's **impairment** and how it affects their ability to do the sport. The different classes keep the events fair. Some athletes use special equipment. For example, they might use a **prosthetic** leg or a wheelchair.

 In the 2016 Paralympic Games, there were 177 events.

There is a lot of racing in athletics. On the track, racers zoom to the finish line. The shortest race is 100 meters long. There are relay races, too. These are teams of racers who take turns running around the track. On the road, racers compete in a marathon. This race is 26.2 miles (42.2 km) long! It takes a lot of **endurance**.

U.S. David Brown races with his guide to qualify for the Paralympics.

An athlete from Azerbaijan chucks a heavy, metal ball in shot put.

 How do **visually impaired** athletes know where to throw and when to jump?

Inside the track there is a field for throwing events. Athletes try to throw balls, discs, and spears the farthest. There are also jumping events. In some events, athletes jump as far as they can. In others, a bar is set. Athletes try to jump over the bar without touching it. The highest jump wins.

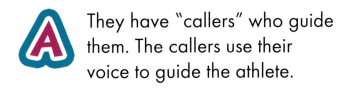

They have "callers" who guide them. The callers use their voice to guide the athlete.

Cycling

Whoosh! Cyclists fly by. Paralympic cycling is a fast sport. Each sport class uses a different bike. Some athletes use bicycles. Others race on tricycles, which have three wheels. Athletes in wheelchairs usually bike with handcycles. They pedal with their arms. Visually impaired cyclists use **tandem bikes**. They pedal behind a guide who can see and steer.

 Do guides receive a medal if they win?

A Dutch athlete speeds around a corner in a handcycle event.

 Yes! Guides on tandem bikes have received medals since 2008. Since 2012, all guides have received the same medal the athlete wins.

Road cycling has three types of events. In the road race, cyclists begin at the same time. The cyclist who finishes first wins. In a **time trial**, cyclists start at different times. Each cyclist is timed. The fastest time wins. The last event is the mixed team relay. Only handcycles are used in this event.

A German handcyclist raises her arms as she finishes a race.

Cycling events also take place on a track. The track is called a **velodrome**. Its sides are steeply angled up. This helps the cyclists make faster turns. Cyclists zoom around the track. Bicycles and tandem bikes are used. There are time trials, pursuit events, and team sprints. Fans sit around the track and cheer.

Cyclists on a tandem bike lean into a turn on a velodrome track.

A British athlete aims a
compound bow at a target.
She gets two shots.

 How far away is the target?

Archery

An archer lifts her bow. She pulls back an arrow and aims. A target is in the distance. It is a circle with ten rings. The closer the arrow lands to the center, the more points the archer scores. The archer releases the arrow. It flies through the air. Thud. It lands in the center. Ten points! Paralympic archery is about precision and accuracy.

 Either 50 or 70 meters away, depending on the event.

There are two types of bows in Paralympic archery. One is a recurve bow. It's the traditional bow. The other is a compound bow. It has pulleys to make it easier to pull the arrow back. In individual events, archers compete two at a time. They take turns shooting at their own targets.

An athlete from Iran releases an arrow from a recurve bow.

British athlete Alison Patrick and her guide rush out of the water in the triathlon.

Q Do transition times count toward the overall race time?

Triathlon

The **triathlon** joined the Paralympic Games in 2016. This race has three parts. It begins with a 750-meter swim. Athletes swim in open water. Next, athletes bike 12.4 miles (20 km) on a road. The race ends with a 3.1 mile (5 km) run to the finish line. The athletes quickly transition between each part.

 Yes. Athletes train to transition quickly. Their gear is all laid out. They put it on the same way each time.

Athletes can use special equipment to help them race. Some use handcycles for the bike ride and racing wheelchairs for the run. Other athletes use a prosthetic leg or arm. Visually impaired athletes use tandem bikes. They also have a guide throughout the race.

Two handcyclists race against each other in the 2016 triathlon.

Future Paralympics

Tokyo, Japan will host the Summer Paralympic Games in 2020. There will be many individual sports to watch. The events in this book will be included. You can also watch canoe, swimming, powerlifting, and more. For action-packed sports, don't miss the Paralympics!

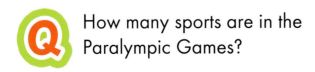

How many sports are in the Paralympic Games?

Para athletes celebrate winning medals in a cycling event.

 In 2020, there will be 22. Of these, 10 can be played individually.

Glossary

disability A physical or mental condition that limits a person's movements, senses, or activities.

endurance The ability to keep doing something for a long time.

impairment A difference in a person's body structure or function, or mental function.

individual One person.

prosthetic An artificial body part, such as an arm or a leg.

sport class In Paralympic sports, a group of athletes with impairments that similarly impact their ability to do a sport.

tandem bike A bike designed to sit two people. The second cyclist sits directly behind the first.

time trial A competition where athletes race individually and their time is scored. The best time wins.

triathlon A race in which athletes swim, bike, and run.

velodrome An indoor cycling track that has steep walls.

visually impaired An impairment that affects a person's ability to see.

Read More

Fullman, Joe. *Going for Gold: A Guide to the Summer Games*. London: Wayland, 2016.

Osborne, M. K. *Track and Field*. Summer Olympic Sports. Mankato, Minn.: Amicus, 2020.

Websites

Olympics | Paralympic Games: History
https://www.olympic.org/paralympic-games

Paralympics | Sports
https://www.paralympic.org/sports/summer

Toyko 2020 | Paralympic Sports—Athletics
https://tokyo2020.org/en/games/sport/paralympic/athletics/

Index

About the Author

Matt Bowers is a writer and illustrator who lives in Minnesota. When he's not writing or drawing, he enjoys skiing, sailing, and going on adventures with his family. As a sports fan, he looks forward to the 2020 Paralympic Games in Tokyo, Japan!